Don't Lose Your Head

" ... the children of suicides
are hard to please and quick
to believe no one loves them
because they are not really here."

--Toni Morrison, "Jazz"

Don't Lose Your Head

Jeanette Powers

EMP Books
Toledo, OH
empbooks.com

1st Edition: 11 7 5 3 2 1
ISBN: 978-0-9985077-4-3
LLOC: 2017945514

This book is a work of fiction. Names, characters, places, dates, and incidents are products of the author's imagination, or are used fictitiously, satirically, or as parody. Any resemblance to actual persons, living or dead, business establishments, events, or locales is entirely coincidental.

Design, Layout, and Interior Art:
Jeanette Powers
Edits, cover design: Ezhno Martin

Table of Contents

(to my father,
William Milford Burns
and to his best friend
Ricky Charles Dodson)

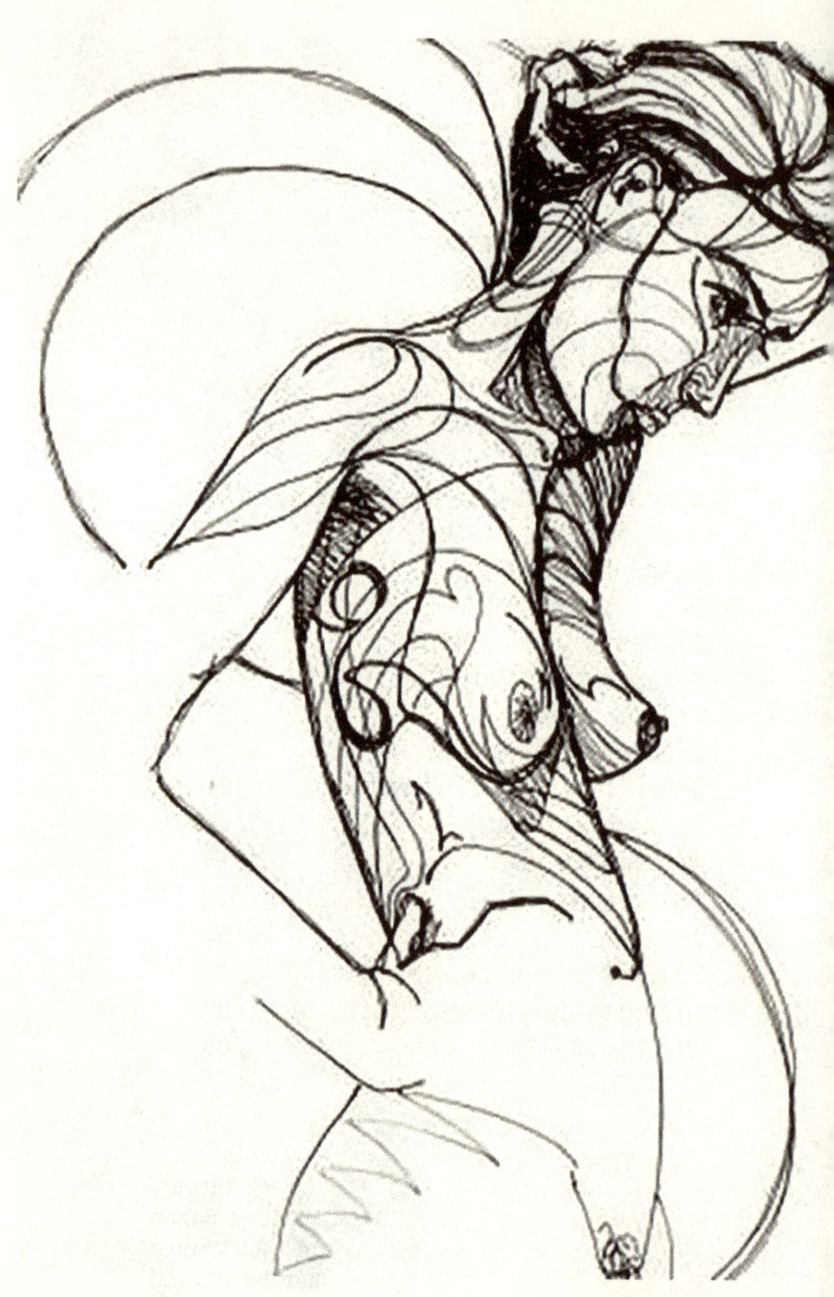

Decapitation: father

her father was both
David and Goliath
the small, the charmed, the Chosen
the warrior, the terrifying one
the Beast,
and like the end of that tale
someone ended up Losing His Head

ended up with
his head on the ground

bodiless

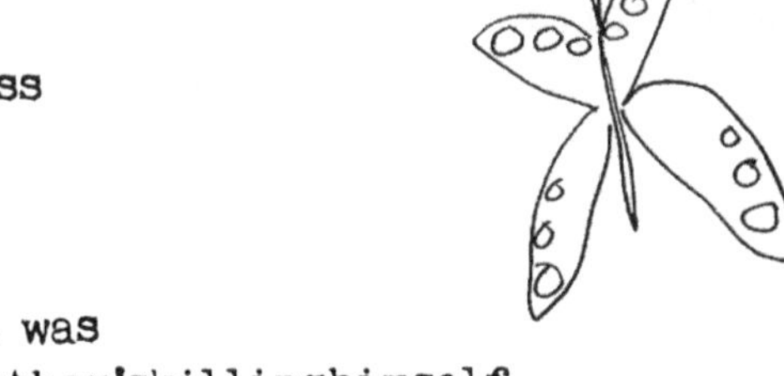

but it was
her father'skillinghimself
by snorting lines of coke
off a mirror next to his fiance
in his convertible Porsche
at 10 a.m.
driving
(reckless)
around Wyandotte County Lake
and bending down to snort it up
his elbow nudged the wheel
flipped his sports car

and he lost control

broken-
ness

I
was
stand-
ing

(you
were
there)

then
I
fell
down.

There
was
no
reason
to
have

f
a
l
l
e
n

except
there
was

a
snap.

One
didn't
know
then
how
one'd
always
had
a
gasp
c
a
u
g
h
t
in
the
back
of
one's
neck.

becamethePavement
circling that Lake
with fishing holes
boat ramps
and a dog park

and where west 93rd Lane
meets Shelter 8
was where that drive

(car rolling, no seatbelt
holding him in)

that drive
took off
his beLOVEd head

heights
stairs
ice
wet
sur-
faces
walking
balance
mostly,

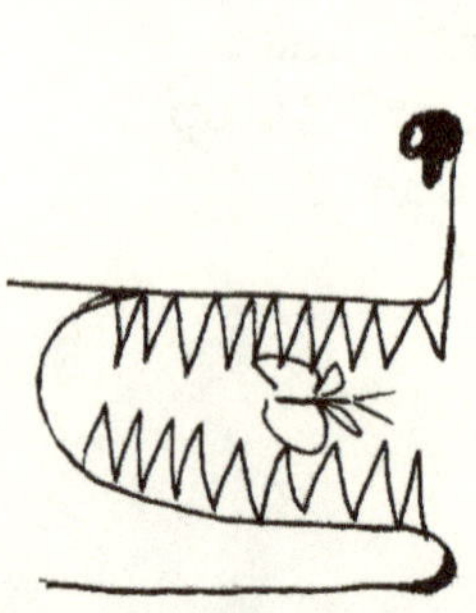

Things you don't know about me: embarrassing

In order to be a child with
the embarrassing death of a parent,
the adults will decide to lie to one
and not tell the little innocent
about what really happened,
instead to tell one
as little as possible
about what happened.

They will not take one
to the funeral,
they will not take one
to the wake.

They will avoid people who knew
what really happened for weeks,
weeks which sometimes will
turn into years,
to avoid that person accidentally
telling one
what really happened.

The adults in one's life
will develop
a habit of not talking
about one's dead father
because
it's hard to lie to a child

(I
don't
like
people
being
too
close)

one
might
never
forgive
a
broken
prom-
ise.

bs
oe
n
so
bro
sneek
knee
bee
k
ken
seek
see
ness
s

what
hap-
pened?

I
broke
my
leg.

I
was
stand-
ing,
then
I
fell.

no
one
could
fathom
how
taking
one
step
could
shatter
one
into
pieces.

(don't
lose
your
head
it's ok
if
you
die)

and because they are grieving, too,
and it's easier sometimes
to avoid talking at all
when talking might revealtoomuch
about how he died,
and how it affected everyone,
and everyone will teach one
about THE GOOD of moving on.

In order to be a child with
the embarrassing death of a parent,
one will not realize
that one's father's death
was embarrassing
one will just understand
that this is a thing
no one talks about
and one will wordlessly feel
there must be some reason
for not talking about death,
about him,
and one will become afraid
to ask about him at all
and one will grow up with a void
for a father,
one will avoid thinking about
having a father,
one will become an existentialist,
one won't believe
one really exists,
one will be hard to please
as a ghost is hard to please

one will feel perhaps
that one should not be
talking about oneself, either.

In order to be a child with
the embarrassing death of a parent,
one must watch
other fathers doing things
(and not doing things)))))))))))))))))))))))))))))))))
with their children
and one will develop an idea
that one is alienated from everyone,
this will make one become
both inventive and somehow
thankful.

The inventive part will imagine
how wonderful and famous
one's father would have been,
how perfect one's life
would have been
had one had a father:

with impetuous heart,
catamaraning about
and blowing glass on horseback.

One will watch other fathers
and be embarrassingly thankful
that one's father is in a position
to never hurt one,
he will never have to say

the dr.
said I
would
break
bones
for
the
rest
of
my
life
.
.
.
.
.
17
so,
so far.

One
began
believ-
ing
new
things
about
the
world

one:
that
one
was
dead.

dead.
dead.
dead.
dead.
dead.
dead.
dead.
dead.
dead.
dead.
dead.
dead.
dead.
dead.
dead.
dead.
dead.
dead.
dead.
dead.
dead.
dead.
dead.
dead.
dead.
dead.
dead.
dead.
dead.
dead.
dead.
d d
e
a a
d d

"I'm sorry",
he will never do one any harm
besides,
of course,
the ongoing absence.

One will go for MANY YEARS
before it dawns on one
that one has the power to ask

pOWerful questions

and that one
has never felt
the death of one's-----------father
so profoundly
until one moment
where one
realizes,
one doesn't know
anything
about one's dad
or how he died
and one uses
the telephone
and one calls
the father's
best friend
and asks

"what happened?".

INTERSTITIAL: CARRY ON

The "Carry On" franchise primarily consists of a sequence of 31 low-budget British comedy motion pictures (1958-92), four Christmas specials, a television series of thirteen episodes, and three West End and provincial stage plays. The films' humour was in the British comic tradition of the music hall and bawdy seaside postcards. The theme song went like this:

Don't Lose Your Head. Don't lose your head when you can't pay your taxes. Don't lose your head when they're grinding their axes. Try to calm when your head's on the block... you may be in for a nasty shock. Don't lose your head, get a hold of your wig, Smile when the gravedigger's swords start to dig. Don't lose your head, you'll get by in the end, Don't lose your head, my friend. Don't lose your head when they're screaming for blood. Don't lose your head or your name will be mud. You're asking for trouble if you know head, cause when you wake up, YOU'LL BE DEAD.

Don't lose your head when the world's at its worst. Don't lose your head when the bubble has burst.

like father like daughter

One began believing that if one left the house the weight of the atmosphere would crush one's bones to dust.

One would call it crush injury

and
how.

crush
in-
jury
bs
srk
ne
ss
boss
reek
brenk
one
sober
sons
seen
broke
nose

it's ok

(you
were
there
two
worlds
col-
lided)

eek
nee
see
n
no

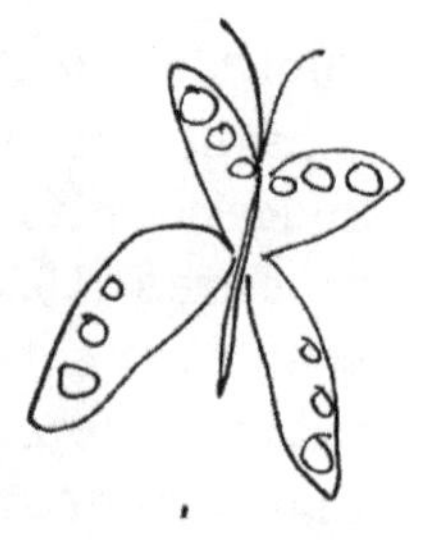

Don't lose your head,
you'll get by in the end.

Don't lose your head, my friend.
Don't Lose Your Head, my friend.

YOU'LL
BE
DEAD.

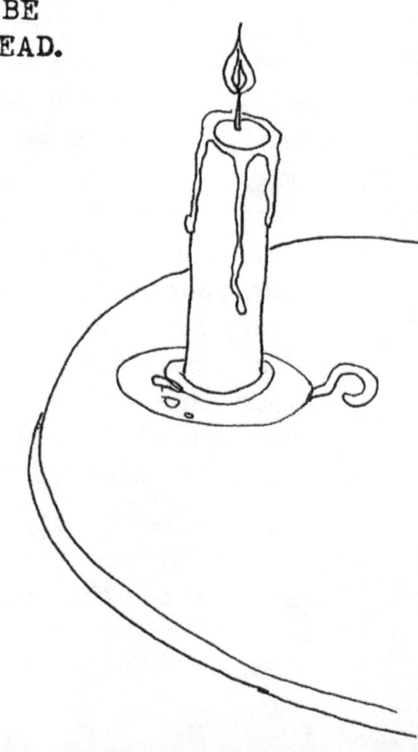

Decapitation: knocked up

Her mother was nothing more
than a little-poor-white-trash-girl
without a dream
or idea in her head,
but she was sosososososososososo (sos)
so beautiful.

Still, it doesn't take a genius
to want to be LOVEd
and being vacant
nevertheless
didn't stop her
from having these
feelings and falling
madly wildly for a man,
man she was
head over heels in L.O.V.E.
(even though
none of us will use that
turn of phrase anymore)
heaDOverheelsheAdoverheels
after the Lake and the Road
and how he LOST His Head
but Samson did not LOVE Delilah
because she was
mundane
and because he was wild
andbrilliantandheavenlyandbrave
and she couldn't take that

see
no
keen
bs

crush
in-
jury
srk
oe
n
so
bro
sneek
knee
bee
k
seek
see
k
n
k
r
sne
nkr
nk
r

I
love
your
pre-
cious
heart

star
fuck
my
brain
broke.

I
was
stand-
ing,
then
I
fell.

One
held
a
dozen
funer-
als for
one's
dead
self
mean-
while
all
that
re-
mained
was
a
LONE
hateful
voice
in

being more born to
clip coupons
research the best price
on a new dining set
nevertheless
it's not too hard
to knock back a bottle of tequila
on New Year's Eve night
and get Knocked Up
not too hard to push
another head
out from between
your two legs

PUSH OUT a little girl
she don't want into this world
unless Samson wanted
that little girl
and Delilah's hand in marriage.

Course that's not what happened
father said NOWAYJOSE
and so our orphan,
our her,
our she,
our Dorothy GaletornadoLife
how she came to be
a product
of a
one-
night-
stand.

Things you don't know about me:
astronaut

When I was a kid
I decided to be an astronaut.

In order to be an astronaut
one must know about stars and space,
how to make small spaces safe,
how to breathe slowly
and not react too fast
and to react just right
or else one would get more hurt.

One must know
about planets and gravity
and lift-off,
one will dream every day about
getting away
into the vast quiet empty.

In order to be an astronaut
one must dig through bookstores
one finds star maps,
national geographic photo specials
one finds Isaac Asimov
and Carl Sagan,
these men will teach
a fatherless girl
what it is to be a man
teach one to take a problem apart

one's
head.
It
was
always
saying:

don't
do
that,
idiot
end-
lessly
needing
to
be
grudg-
ing,
cor-
recting,
better
not
break
any-
thing

every-
thing
moves
so
so
so
so
so
fast

bore
sre
sker
so
ne
oee
ken

One
was
scared
of
every-
thing

sud-
denly
and
so,
so
a
a
a
angry
until
one
saw
the
real
crush
injury
had
been
long
ago.

piece by piece
teach one to look at what
one really sees
and to ignore
what one expects to see
because observing a thing
changes that thing.

One learns about the chance of life
on other planets,
places so unlike this place
one might not even
recognize
the strange
alien
life.

In order to be an astronaut
one must have a telescope
and one must
learn to edge the grass
and feed the dog
and save the clinking
quarters from chores
for a universe of time
(all summer).

Then,
one learns the heady rush
of the name Bushnell
and one sneaks away
on particularly dark nights

to the hill at the park
twists the distances
of perfect lenses,
squints slightly,
and brings something
like Saturn
right to one's eyes,
and one learns
to leave
the grips of the 'scope loose
if one is gonna watch
the moon,
because
it moves so,
so
fast.

No
one
told
me
about
how
my
father
LOST
his
head.

About
or-
phan-
s.

How
can
some-
one
re-
press
so
so
much?

I
was
stand-
ing

(you
were
there)

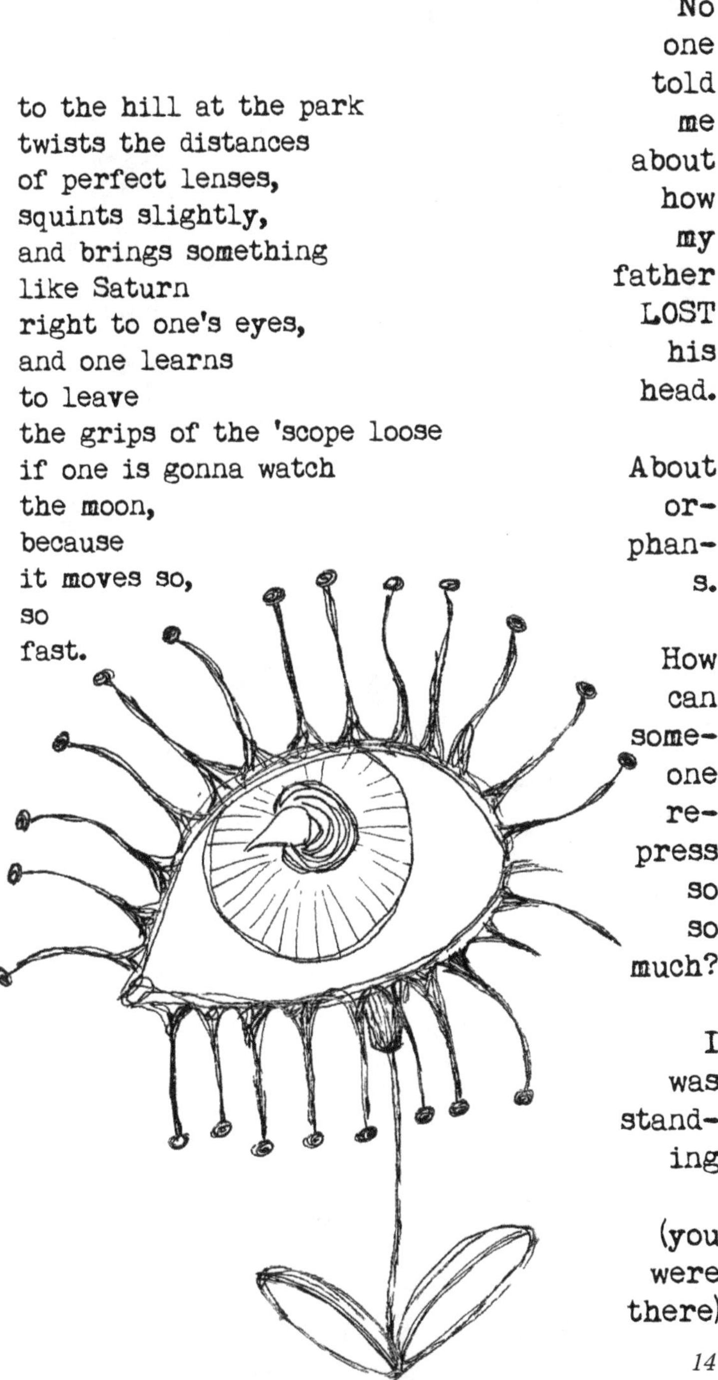

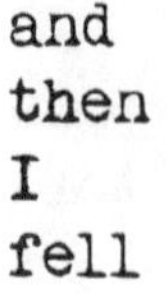

and
then
I
fell

I
broke
my
leg
into
5
pieces

crush
in-
jury.
dead.
dead.
dead.
dead.
dead.
dead.
dead.
dead.
dead.
dead.
dead.
dead.
dead.
dead.
dead.
dead.
dead.
dead.
dead.

i
will
be
perfect
if

"You wake up
in the morning
with a starfuck
for a friend."

it
kills
me

INTERSTITIAL: INXS

"Don't Lose Your Head" is the third single from the album "Elegantly Wasted" by INXS. No official release for this in USA. The song was written by Michael Hutchence and Andrew Farriss and recorded by the band in Dublin during the summer of 1996. INXS released "Don't Lose Your Head" as a promo tie-in with Paramount's 1997 film "Face/Off" starring John Travolta and Nicolas Cage. The opening lines to the song had to be rewritten, the original lines went as such:

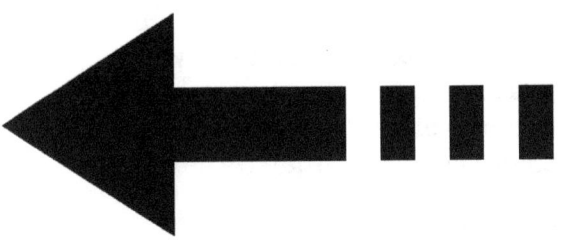

INXS was the first cassette tape Dorothy owned. Karen, a long-haired welder friend of Delilah's bought the tape for her from a Walmart in the suburbs.

It's not true that they could never tear us apart.

I
LOST
my
head.

Bro-
ken-
ness-
ago-
bs-
srk-
oe-
n-
so-
bro-
sneek-
knee-

I
am
brok-
en

I
a
m
b
r
o
k
e
n
w
h
o

l
l
y
b
r
o
s
s
e
n
e
k
o
r
b

new
orb
ma

I
am
broken

ness

deeply
sad
about
loss
about
how
my
dog
can

Decapitation: Delilah

The next time
mother LOST her head
was because Samson LOST his
and so she married
the next man
with money, a real DALE EARNHARDt
fastmoney$$$$$$$$$$$$$
and fell into a hole
the size of the pour spout
of a bottle of vodka
maybe it was Hot DAMN.

I don't know her drink of choice
although today I'll tell you
it's beer and wine
because she's learned
that the elixirs go to her head
so,
so fast.

She's had to
(well, should have had to)
say sorry too much.

Instead of doing that (sayingsorry)
she just keeps her eyes
shifty
and doesn't speak so much
unless it's to blame someone else.

You can tell the mark of a person
who believes they're innocent
because every time you accuse them
of something, they go and point
the blame on someone else.

The truly guilty
are the ones who
know they're guilty,
and they just say
they're sorry, (if they are)
if they're not,
they'll just say:
"fuck you."
"fuck you."
"fuck you."
"fuck you."
"fuck you."
"fuck you."
"fuck you."
"fuck you."
"fuck you."
"fuck you."
"fuck you."
"fuck you."
"fuck you."
"fuck you."
"fuck you."
"fuck you."
"fuck you."
"fuck you."
"get over it."

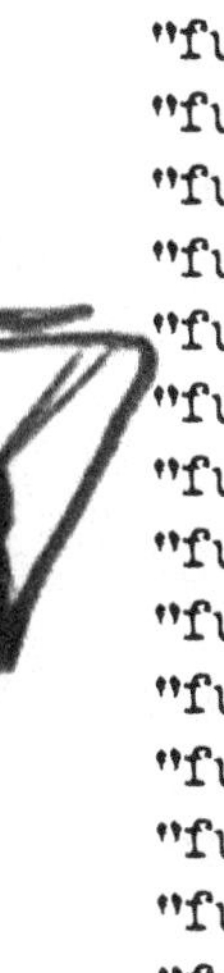

sleep
so
well
thr-
ough
pain
about
how
adopted
chil-
dren
are
want-
ed
by
their
new

parents
about
how
amnesia
gives
you
a
new
life
about
how
babies
smell
about
not
being
able

to
leap
into
the
river
and
be
swept
home

I
was
stand-
ing.

then

I
fell
down.

there
was
no
reason
to
have

f
a
l
l
e
n

Admission: highlander

o hai bitch
u inauguratedeverything
about me elected to neglect me
& u should be proud
because I
done more than you could even ream

u lied to 'em,
2 me,
ur made of erased search history

u ctrl alt del ctrl h
u don't care
but I'm bout to hardcopy
this shittin away u could'd
never imagined because I understand

(fuck)
thatyouhavebeenhurt

ur father madeyoufeel worthless
ur othermadeyou subservient
ur brother was fatanorexic
ur sister was sugardiabetic
everyone starveburned or
ate-hid-gnawed
their feelings, everyone went
blankhead

blanket

ur dogs were coweredobedient
ur father LOVEd thosedogs so
godDAMNEDhard
that it made youwanttobe obedient

u were so beautifulthatyou
thoughthat
was
all
that
mattered

and youo thaougt taht
bkase u were wthe
ahlhwleysnmost
beaugfitufl womanintehw
worls thatnotthing

thhoyoutoculneedaodoawnatweven
paieceshitblitelecunt t
dnotbe tsomethign worthfrgavn

except
there
was
a
snap.

And
I
was
torn
apart.

One
didn't
know
then
how
one'd
always
had
a
gasp

c
a
u
g
h
t

in
the
back
of
one's

neck.

what
hap-
pend?
?
?
?
?
?
?
?
?
?
?
?
?
?
(I
don't
like
people
being
too
close)
?
?
?
?
?
?
?
?
?
one

Decapitation: sister

Mother did the best she could
by marrying that rich man
and to his benefit
he probably really LOVEd her,
not that he could continue
loving someone who hated him
and was only using him
but that's all
that poor little white trash girls
really know, right?

Maybe that's all most people
really know, right?

But he was a liar and a thief
in his own right, a race car driver

(funny how she might long for a man
who could handle a hairpin curve
while snorting a line of coke
without Losing His Head).

He was a two-bit truck stop Bandit
taking semi-trailers full of
packages back home so we had
not one
but ten thousand
Mickey Mouse telephones
the summer of 1982.

That was the year sister was born.
The second child. The first one
was wanted to catch her first LOVE
and the second one was unneeded
cuz she already had a man.

Mother was pissed.
Mother who was angry.
Mother didn't intend to get
Knocked Up
and mother spent nine (9) months off
the bottle (probably)
hating on that child
hating on that child
so hard
she daily cursed at her womb.

Mother who nearly caused that child
to lose her head because
when the nurses had her feet up
high in the stirrups
in the labor pains
in the sweat of her beautiful
blonde hair plastered
across her face turning her
into some kind of sea-kelp
Nightmare and shewasScreaming
for the death of everybody
she ever knew
the nurse cried

STOP

might
never
forgive

a
broken
prom
ise.
bs
srk
oe
n
so
bro
sneek
knee
bee
k
seek
see
k
n
k
r
sne
nkr
nk
r
sn
e
be
so
keen
one
bone

kone
one
om
on
orb
sore
or
sre
I
broke
my
leg.

I
was
stand-
ing,
then
I
fell.

Did
you
love
me?

"I
don't
know."

No
one
could
fathom
how

STOP

My mother cried FUCK YOU

and then they said "stop
or
you're going to kill this child."

I can't imagine how hard
it would be to close your legs
at that point
but mother did save the baby
her umbilical cord
was wrapped around her neck
9 times
and the birthing process
almost strangled her
and mother's had to live
every day ever since
knowing her wish
for that child
to be dead

did its dirty work
in the womb.

taking
one
step
could
shatter
one
into
pieces.

One
began
believ-
ing
new
things
about
the
world.
one:
that
one
was
dead.

two:
that
one
was
dead.

three:
that
one
was
dead.

Things you don't know about me: protector

I couldn't protect my sister.
In order to protect one's sister
one did in fact,
sit at her bedroom door
while reading A Tale of 2 Cities
Jane Eyre, CUjo
and THe SHining
so he'd see one was there
and know he couldn't pass
the threshold to her bed,
(like he'd trespassed into one's)
but one's sister had already
been abused by others,
namely mother ...
not that sister'd see it until
years later when her husband said
"we won't raise our children
the way you were raised"
and sister was confused,
(but one knew)
and one was thankful
for sister's husband
who somehow innocently verified
what one had been saying
all these long years.

But back to where one began,
one sat at her doorstop

YOU'LL
BE
DEAD.

it's ok

One
began
believ-
ing
that
the
weight
of
the
atmo-
sphere
would
crush
one's
bones
to
dust.

One
would
call
it
crush
injury
but
not
know
that
what

to stop that step-father from
entering her door
even though one didn't understand
then that the step-father
had a penchant for
12-year-olds
and not for 1st graders.

In order to protect one's sister,
one would have to invent
a time machine and travel back
to when one was an only child,
and it would take one many years
to parse back the incidents
and realize
that one's mother didn't want
another child but just wanted
someone to take care of her
and even
when one's mother found out
about younger sister in utero,
one's mother hated that sibling
as much as she hated the first
and one could never turn back
the wheels to make one's mother
LOVE
the second child
any more than one could make
the mother LOVE the first.

But, one's mother's hatred
of the second child would end

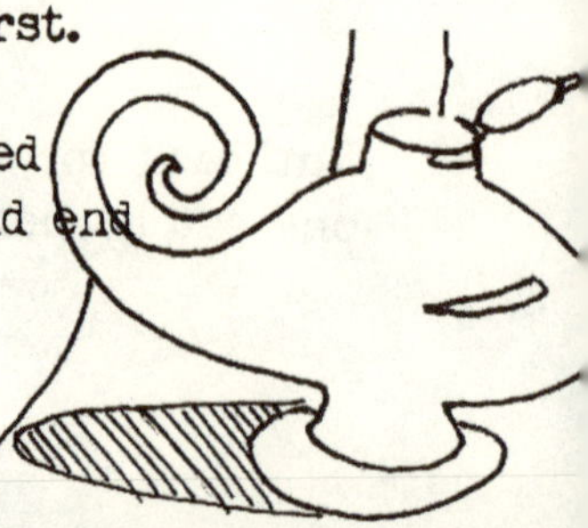

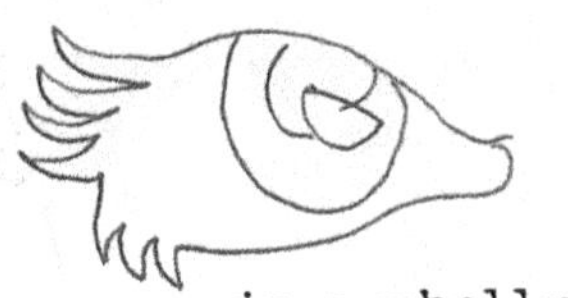

in a wholly different way.

One's sister would be born
with her umbilical cord
wrapped around her neck
9 times. (9)(9)(9)(9)(9)(9)(9)(9)(9)(9)(9)(9)

One's sister would nearly
be strangled upon delivery.
Furthermore, one's sister
would be born with cross-eyes
and a hole in her heart,
but most dramatically
one's sister would be born
with club feet
both feet turned 270 degrees
off the foreward march position
which meant she might never walk
and what's worse is that one
& one's own mother
would both always know
that all of this deformity
was because one's mother
never LOVEd but only used
& one's mother would feel guilty,
so guilty she'd divorce
and marry a rich rapist
and divorce and marry
another rich man on hope
because that was mother's way
and new man (#4) would supposedly
salvage all the broken everything

doctor
kennedy
would
call
it
was
dis-
socia-
tion
and
how
I
was
dead
for
a
solid
three
months,
like
father
like
daugh-
ter.

bs
srk
ne
ss
boss
reek
brenk
one
sober
sons

"you
never
did
know
when
to
shut
your
fucking
mouth"

I
disso-
ciated
for
years

the
helmet
pro-
tected
against
a
head
shot
which
was
fatal

like
father
like
daugh-
ter
like

of two abused children
but really he just
ended up being another
of mother's victims
(he used to laugh so easily).

In order to protect my sister,
one'd have to wait years
uponyearsuponyears until
the moment that sister
had perspective to see
her (our) (one's)
mother was human.

One'd have to wait until
sister was pregnant,
until a child sister
would protect came along,
a child to guard
as one had guarded
sister's door,
her chasm,
until she
would do
the same
for another.

The way one's
mother
would never
do for either
of them.

Decapitation: feral child

Little girl LOST her head
every day when mother came home
drunk after work
after little girl
had made her own dinner
made religion of turkey-pot-pies
and cherished the occasional
Big Mac the neighbor brought her
because she knew she was all alone.

She LOST her head as her mother
called her "little filthy
disgusting cunt"
told her she was worthless
told her she cost her everything
told her she wasted her youth
on having this Little Orphan Child
(funny years later mother would
ask to take Dorothy's first born
so one could have fun in her 20's
but also so mother could do better
the second (third) time around).

Mother LOST her head
because she couldn't remember
a thing for 14 years
and when the little girl
turned woman, she would ask her
to fill out a senior paper for

it's ok
it's
ok
it's ok
it's
ok
it's ok
it's
ok
it's ok
it's
ok
it's ok
it's
ok
it's ok
it's
ok
it's ok
it's
ok
it's ok
it's
ok
it's ok
it's
ok
it's ok
it's
ok
it's ok
it's
ok
it's ok
it's

ok

it's
ok
to
die

star
fuck

(cuz
we
all
have
wings

but

some
of
us
don't
know
why)

Some-
thing
in-
side
me
broke
I
was
all
alone.

Mother's Day which one's teacher
made them write where
one interviews the mother
about what it was like raising one
and the paper was supposed to be
eight pages but wouldn't be
more than two paragraphs.

She said "I remember
the vacation to Disneyland
I remember that we went to dinner
at your grandma and grandpa's.
I remember you like dogs
and that I got you a bike once."

What was one's first word?
"I don't know"

What was one like as a child?
"You were awful."

What was one's favorite thing to do?
"I don't know."

Did I have a lot of friends?
"I don't know."

Was I good in school?
"I don't know."

Did you LOVE me?

INTERSTITIAL: DEFINITION

"Lose Head"

Idiom Definition. Your browser does not support the audio element.
"to lose your head" : to become angry or confused or emotional to the point where you cannot think clearly.

category: body and bodily functions.

The phrase alludes to the fact that our emotions, thinking ability and self control are regulated in the head. The exact origin is unclear, however, it was definitely known and in use by the late 19th century.

Don't lose your head,
you'll get by in the end.

Don't lose your head, my friend.
Don't Lose Your Head, my friend.

YOU'LL
BE
DEAD.

broken-
ness

I
was
stand-
ing

(you
were
there)

then
I
fell
down.

there
was
no
reason
to
have

f
a
l
l
e
n

except
there
was

a
snap.

One
didn't
know
then
how
one'd
always
had
a
gasp
c
a
u
g
h
t
in
the
back
of
one's
neck.

heights
stairs
ice
wet
sur-
faces
walking
balance
mostly,

Decapitation: Dorothy

Dorothy followed in both
her parents footsteps.

One by being bright
and willful and wild
two by falling down
into a bottle of whisky
or Bailey's or opium
or whatever else went her way,
course she had daddy issues.

Question: did she marry a man
25 years her senior?
Who knocked her head
into the pavementground
turned her head over Heels
on a daily basis?
Who worked to erase her mind
because that was the only way
he could keep someone
as fine as her
around?
He did have standards you know
it's no good to crush something
useless under your boot heel,

if you're brilliant,
you want to destroy
Something Beautiful.

Things mom doesn't know about me: fever

In order for mother to know me,
first one must sit in the silent
of early dawn
and be so,
so still
the lizards run over one's toes
and the armadillos
trundle past in ignorance
of one's could-be-threatening
and snootily forage
and mother must stare right where
one already knows
the sun will break
over the black trees
and mother must also stare there
into the rising sun
until it seemingly blinds one
and one must
Lose One's Mind
and stay there in the fire
until the dew is dry
and the bright orb is high.

For one who is my mother
to know me,
mother must be told
one's first memory of her:

(I
don't
like
people
being
too
close)

one
might
never
forgive
a
broken
prom-
ise.

bs
oe
n
so
bro
sneek
knee
bee
k
ken
seek
see
ness
s

what
hap-
pened?

I
broke
my
leg.

I
was
stand-
ing,
then
I
fell.

no
one
could
fathom
how
taking
one
step
could
shatter
one
into
pieces.

(don't
lose
your
head
it's ok
if
you
die)

she fighting
with one's sister's father
and one must know
that preschooler
in a Mork hat
made a promise
to one's self that day
that one has felt the undercurrent
of in every day after:

one promised one's self
that the world must be bigger
than this small house
and whatever happened
one-would-never-be-like-mother.

Mother should be reminded
one taught one's self to read
before one ever
darkened the bell
of a classroom door
and mother should know
one felt more at home there.

In order for my mother to know me,
one must remember that
mother is best in pain
and reliable most
when all the houses
have been reduced to rubble
and there is a funeral,
a bedpan,

a climate of catastrophe,
a duty.

Mother doesn't know
how to live in joy,
one must remember
how mother put out the fire
one's brother started in the closet
where he starved,
how mother buried
her two sugar-sick sisters:
one young,
but one after such long illness,
remember
how mother shouldered
the burden of that sister
far past recognition
of self, dog, bug, or sister.

One must remember
the divorces
the broken bones
the hospitals
and the carrying of my body

(which one then believed to be dead)

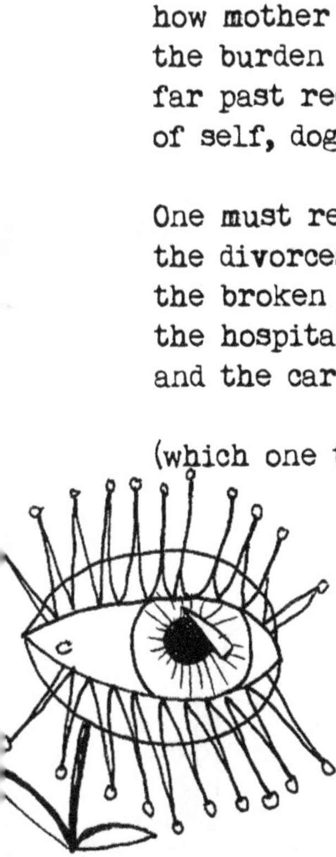

and how when one
was resurrected
that one LOVEd mother,
how when the fever broke
one called out for her.

the dr.
said I
would
break
bones
for
the
rest
of
my
life
.
.
.
.
.
17
so,
so far.

One
began
believ-
ing
new
things
about
the
world

one:
that
one
was
dead.

dead.
dead.
dead.
dead.
dead.
dead.
dead.
dead.
dead.
dead.
dead.
dead.
dead.
dead.
dead.
dead.
dead.
dead.
dead.
dead.
dead.
dead.
dead.
dead.
dead.
dead.
dead.
dead.
dead.
dead.
dead.
d d
e
a a
d d

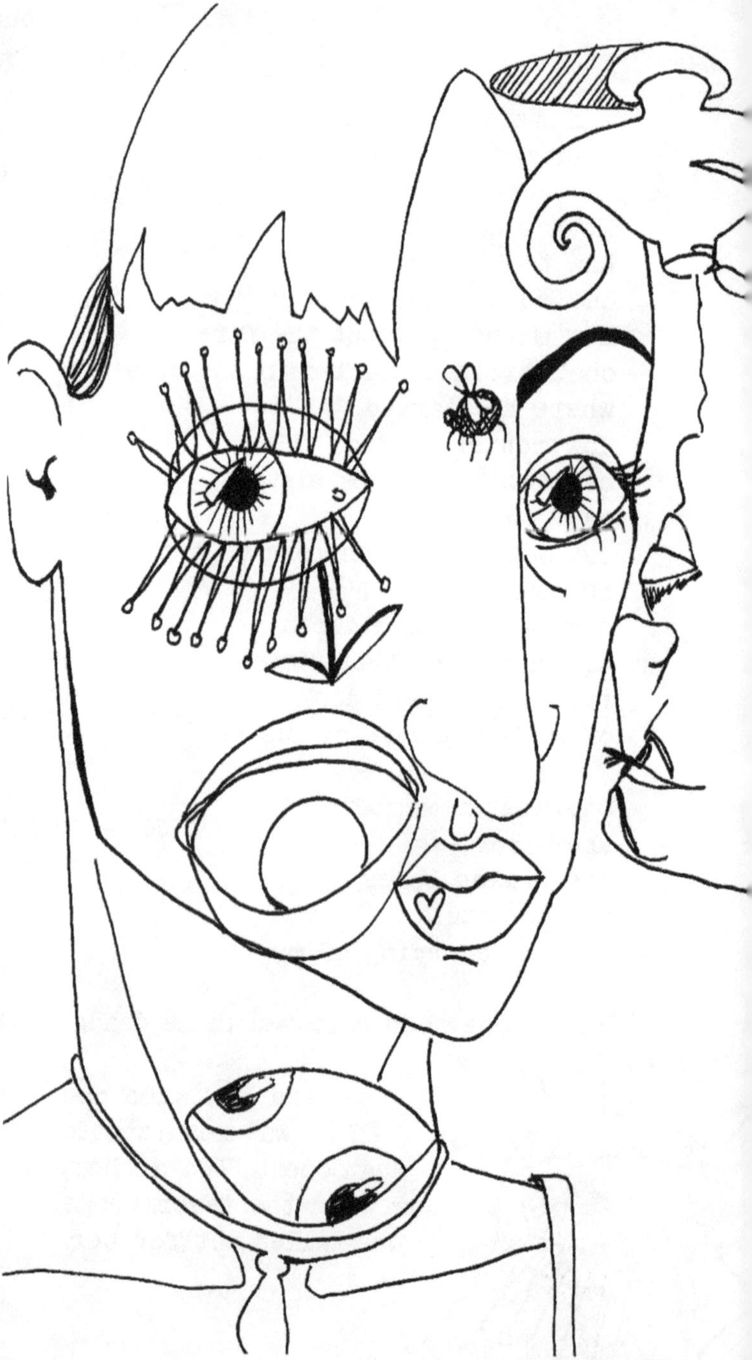

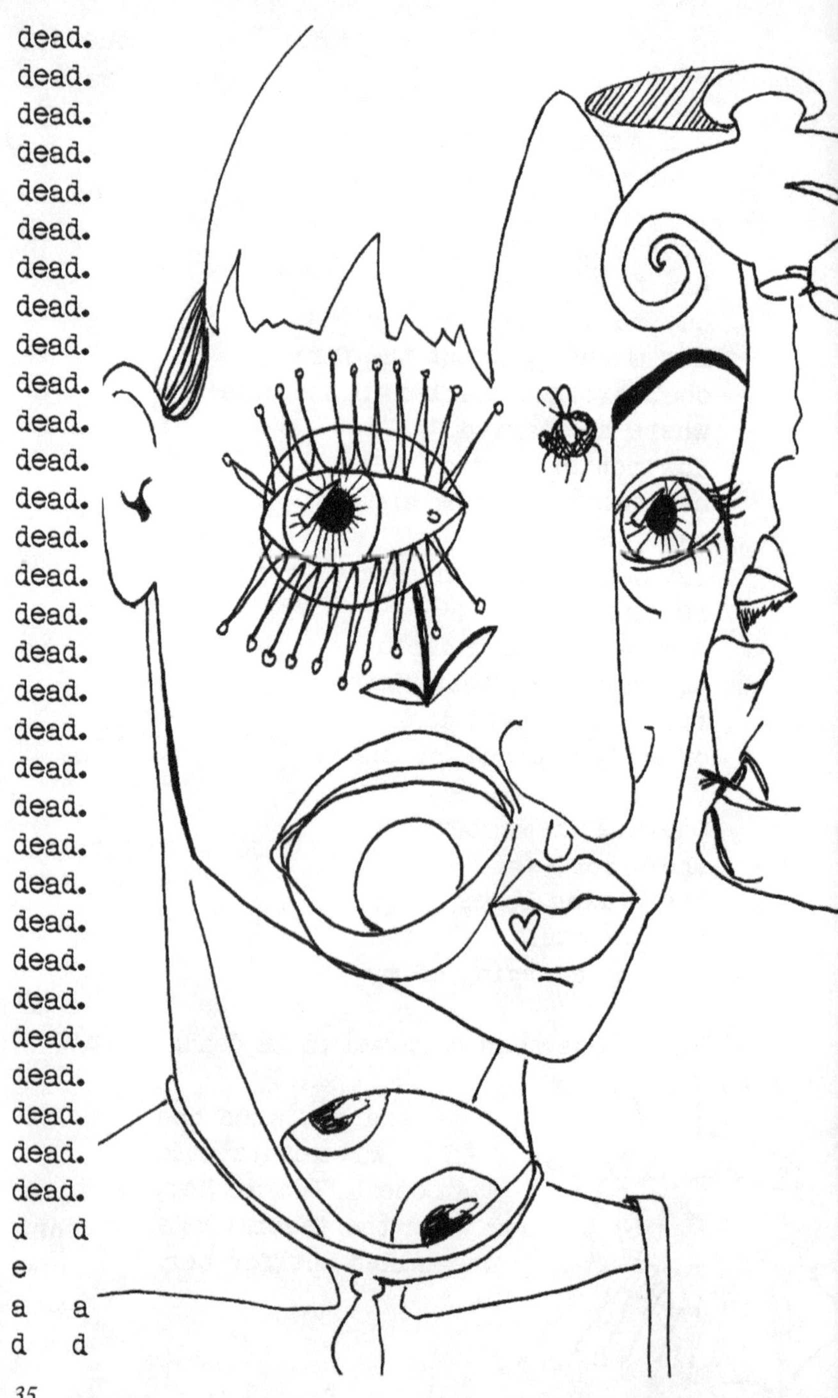

INTERSTITIAL: QUEEN

"A Kind of Magic" is the twelfth studio album by the British rock band Queen, released on 2 June 1986. It was their first studio album to be recorded digitally, and is based on the soundtrack to the film Highlander. "Don't Lose Your Head" is the eighth track on the album and was composed by Taylor and features Joan Armatrading in a vocal cameo. The song takes its name from a line spoken in Highlander, and is played for a short time when Kurgan kidnaps Brenda.

When Freddie Mercury died, Delilah proclaimed to Dorothy, "We didn't know he was gay, back in those days." Dorothy sighed and said "Mom, the band's name was Queen."

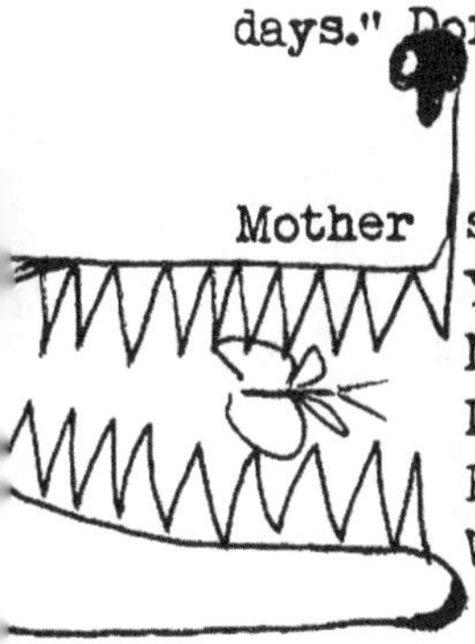

Mother said:
You
Never
Did
Know
When
To
Shut
Your
Fucking
Mouth

like
father
like
daugh-
ter

One
began
believ-
ing
that
if
one
left
the
house
the
weight
of
the
atmo-
sphere
would
crush
one's
bones
to
dust.

One
would
call
it
crush
injury

and
how.

crush
in-
jury
bs
srk
ne
ss
boss
reek
brenk
one
sober
sons
seen
broke
nose

it's ok

(you
were
there
two
worlds
col-
lided)

eek
nee
see
n
no

Decapitation: The Wizard

The German man
who would marry Dorothy
when she was barely twenty
and he was nearly 50
LOST His Head
because he worked in deep Michigan
trolling back roads on a farm
after he legendarily burned down
half-a-city-block in Detroit
because his father
beat him TOO HARD
and the gang members didn't.

Everything has its price
of admission.

So his parents carted him away
to a chicken farm where they were
going to turn things right
the old-fashioned-way,
(through hard work,
without asking for any help)
and there The Wizard was
six-foot-four and strong,
high schooler, brilliant, bright
young man bailing hay
day after day
bailing so much hay it made
a permanent curve in his spine.

see
no
keen
bs

crush
in-
jury
srk
oe
n
so
bro
sneek
knee
bee
k
seek
see
k
n
k
r
sne
nkr
nk
r

I
love
your
pre-
cious
heart

star
fuck
my
brain
broke.

I
was
stand-
ing,
then
I
fell.

One
held
a
dozen
funer-
als for
one's
dead
self
mean-
while
all
that
re-
mained
was
a
LONE
hateful
voice
in

They would stack the bales
high on the tractor after
the afternoon faded and he
would climb to the startling top
of all those bales of hay
and he would sit atop
as the Setting Sun fell
on his face and a moment of wind
rushing through his hair
and a moment of joy away from
the heavy hand of his father
and his histrionic mother
and he didn't notice the truck
took a different way one day.

He didn't notice,
he wasn't looking ahead,
he was looking too much in the sun,
he didn't notice how the phone line
crossed the street just that high
and it caught him in the face
slashed right through
the corner of mouth through cheek
opened his jaw line right up
and that's the first time he LOST
his ability to speak
as his jaw was hanging loose
and he was bleeding out
over the hay bales
as his face fell apart
just thinking about how he
was gonna catch a beating from dad.

Things you don't know about me:
old-man

In order to end an abusive marriage,
one must first admit that one
is just hoping
one's old-man will die.

One will learn to hope for cancer,
or aneurism,
or murder most foul
one will read Hamlet
and dream the 1000 natural shocks,
about being too much in-the-sun,
because one knows that one doesn't
take one's promises lightly.

One will know that this
tragedy involves such other delights
such as forgiving one's own mother
for being a self-absorbed whore
and feeling the deep-buried
loss of one's own father
and come to understand
what daddy-issues really means.

Eventually one will come to see
that some old men know
some young women need a father
figure and have figured out
how to take advantage of them.

one's
head.
It
was
always
saying:

don't
do
that,
idiot
end-
lessly
needing
to
be
grudg-
ing,
cor-
recting,
better
not
break
any-
thing

every-
thing
moves
so
so
so
so
so
fast

bore
sre
sker
so
ne
oee
ken

One
was
scared
of
every-
thing

sud-
denly
and
so,
so
a
a
a
angry
until
one
saw
the
real
crush
injury
had
been
long
ago.

In order to end an abusive marriage,
one must first admit
that one made a mistake
by marrying a man 25 years
her elder
and one must say "thank you"
to her family who
let her make that mistake
and one must say "I'm sorry"
to all the friends he alienated
because he couldn't let
anyone tell the truth
anywhere around him
else he would be exposed
as the child abuser he was
not child, really,
but girl,
still and vulnerable
and weak.
A girl who LOST her head
and fell head-over-heels
fell head over HElls.

One must admit that one
was looking to him
for guidance which he
promised
in this epic sort of way
which made one believe
this old man was more than
some withered wish of what
could-have-been,

and one believed
he had some access
to how homes got built,
cars got fixed,
he bought one a telescope,
he promised he knew
how dreams could be made real.

In order to end an abusive marriage,
one must first be thrown
to the ground in anger
for going out to Princess Diana's
bachelorette party,
and then, one must be
punched in the face for going out
with friends after work
for no reason at all (except maybe
that he already knew
he was too old to go)
and one will forgive
the first incident WAILING

"I know I provoked you"

& one will take a stand
on the second (stating)

"if this happens again, I'll leave"

and in order to end an abusive
marriage one must be raped
in one's own bed

No
one
told
me
about
how
my
father
LOST
his
head.

About
or-
phan-
s.

How
can
some-
one
re-
press
so
so
much?

I
was
stand-
ing

(you
were
there)

and
then
I
fell

I
broke
my
leg
in
4 piec-
es

crush
in-
jury
dead.
dead.
dead.
dead.
dead.
dead.
dead.
dead.
dead.
dead.
dead.
dead.
dead.
dead.
dead.
dead.
dead.
dead.
dead.

by one's own husband
while being threatened
to have one's own child
taken away from them
and one will learn to lie,
there
lie and be raped,
lie, naked, and say

"it's ok"

lie and say:

"I'll do whatever you say."

Promise to homeschool
the offspring, promise to stay home
promise not to go out again,
promise to quit the internet,
promise to be a good girl,
because one will know
that if one makes it to dawn,
one will be able to run away
and run far away
and take one's child
to where one and the child
will be safe
from all the assaults
of that dirty-old-man.

"it's ok."
"it's ok."

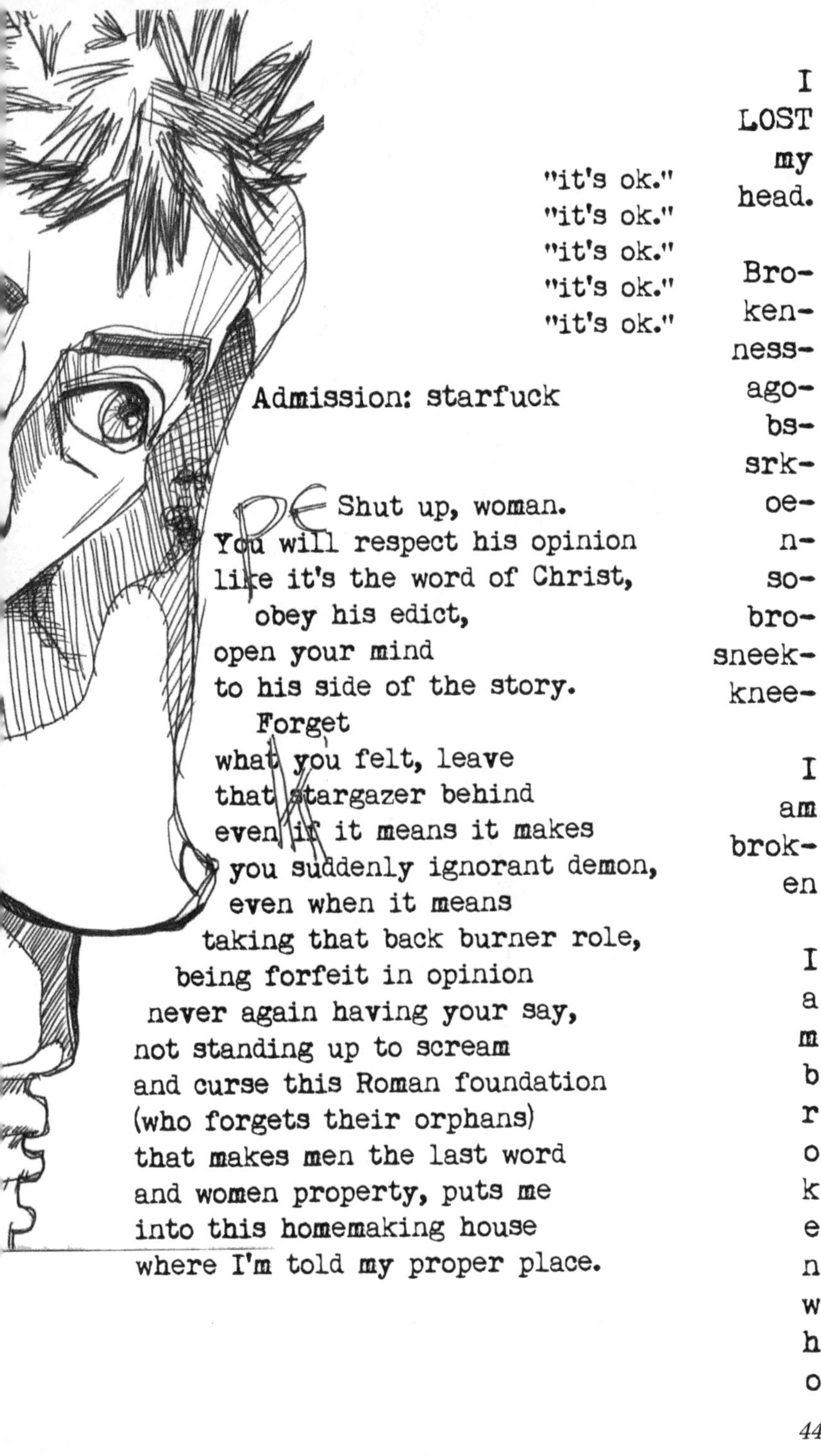

"it's ok."
"it's ok."
"it's ok."
"it's ok."
"it's ok."

Admission: starfuck

Shut up, woman.
You will respect his opinion
like it's the word of Christ,
obey his edict,
open your mind
to his side of the story.
Forget
what you felt, leave
that stargazer behind
even if it means it makes
you suddenly ignorant demon,
even when it means
taking that back burner role,
being forfeit in opinion
never again having your say,
not standing up to scream
and curse this Roman foundation
(who forgets their orphans)
that makes men the last word
and women property, puts me
into this homemaking house
where I'm told my proper place.

I
LOST
my
head.

Bro-
ken-
ness-
ago-
bs-
srk-
oe-
n-
so-
bro-
sneek-
knee-

I
am
brok-
en

I
a
m
b
r
o
k
e
n
w
h
o

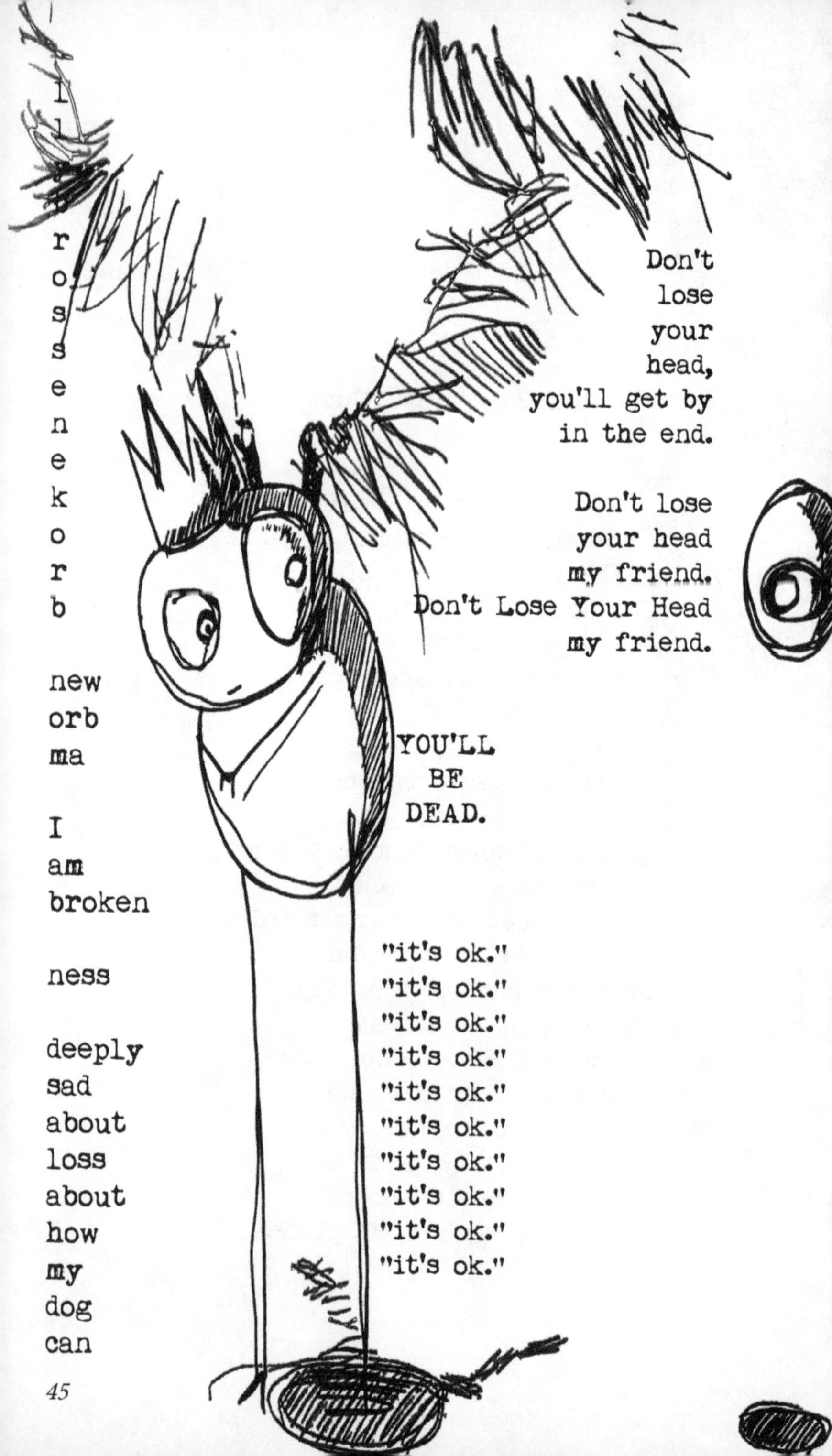

l
l
r
o
s
s
e
n
e
k
o
r
b

new
orb
ma

I
am
broken

ness

deeply
sad
about
loss
about
how
my
dog
can

Don't
lose
your
head,
you'll get by
in the end.

Don't lose
your head
my friend.
Don't Lose Your Head
my friend.

YOU'LL
BE
DEAD.

"it's ok."
"it's ok."
"it's ok."
"it's ok."
"it's ok."
"it's ok."
"it's ok."
"it's ok."
"it's ok."
"it's ok."

Things you don't know about me:
minimums

In order to live a minimal life,
one must not have
a room of their own as a child
one must be a toddler
pawned off on other parents
while one's own mother is off
at god-knows-where
and one must learn
        the courtesy of the couch
one will know that water
is always free,
but that as a guest,
(which is what one is)
everything else must be asked for.

One must master the skill
of being quiet and to hide
without hiding
when the daily-family-dramas
of one's hosts are played out
one must learn
nottocryout for one's mother.

In order to live a minimal life,
one must learn to enjoy being alone
and find one's own way
without burdening others
with too many questions

sleep
so
well
thr-
ough
pain
about
how
adopted
chil-
dren
are
want-
ed
by
their
new

parents
about
how
amnesia
gives
you
a
new
life
about
how
babies
smell
about
not
being
able

to
leap
into
the
river
and
be
swept
home

I
was
stand-
ing.

then

I
fell
down.

there
was
no
reason
to
have

f
a
l
l
e
n

one will find
that one can go quite far past
where the other children
are allowed to go
because one is unchaperoned
and undomesticated
one will discover
that what adults say is dangerous
actually means one no harm at all
and that it is the grown-ups
who are most treacherous,
threatening,
afraid.

One will begin to imagine
one's self more animal
and less human
one will wonder at the stars
and fathom ancestry there
one will develop a lack
of confidence in the answers
of elders.

One will learn not to cry
when asked:
"when is your mother coming back?"
And one will learn to say
"I don't know"
without shame.

In order to lead a minimal life,
one must learn to quickly pack

all of one's belongings at the drop
of a hat, in a single backpack
and choose one pair of shoes,
one book and one toy. One will
choose a choose-your-own-adventure
and a dinosaur named "Wa-meh"
one will learn the words
death, funeral, divorce and move
and one must learn that some things
are more important than others
and things one thought were
indispensable
can be left behind easily
and with little remorse
and that one is not supposed
to talk of the things one LOST.
(good-bye Millenium Falcon, good-bye
Han Solo, good-bye My Little Pony)

In the future,
one will have trouble
remembering most of those things,
find that most things are easily
forgotten and one will eventually
come to understand that one doesn't
even need the backpack ...
That one is complete
in and of one's self
& that there is a kind of baggage
one cannot put down or forget,
& one will decide that those
memories are heavy enough.

except
there
was
a
snap.

And
I
was
torn
apart.

One
didn't
know
then
how
one'd
always
had
a
gasp

c
a
u
g
h
t

in
the
back
of
one's

neck.

what
hap-
pend?
?
?
?
?
?
?
?
?
?
?
?
?
?
(I
don't
like
people
being
too
close)
?
?
?
?
?
?
?
?
?
one

INTERSTITIAL: SERMON

Control Your Thinking (7 of 8)
Defeating the enemy in your life?
by David Cawston
Ephesians 6:10-17

Introduction:
"Take the helmet of salvation ..."

"Keep your head about you."
"Don't lose your head."
The head is one of the most
important organs of the body.
It is the decision center, command
center, observation center, balance
center, thought center, etc.
When you lose your head
you are dead.

No recovery.

First thing David did after he
knocked Goliath down was to cut off
his head.

Notice that the HelMEt is a
defensive piece of clothing.
It only protects.
The helmet protected against a head
shot, which was fatal.

I put on the helmet of salvation
to protect the mind.

might
never
forgive

a
broken
prom
ise.
bs
srk
oe
n
so
bro
sneek
knee
bee
k
seek
see
k
n
k
r
sne
nkr
nk
r
sn
e
be
so
keen
one
bone

kone
one
om
on
orb
sore
or
sre
I
broke
my
leg.

I
was
stand-
ing,
then
I
fell.

Did
you
love
me?

"I
don't
know."

No
one
could
fathom
how

Things you don't know about me: river rat

I swam into the Missouri River.
In order to swim the river
one needs a boat and a paddle
and a rat
river rats are sneaky people
they don't just say
"hey
let me teach you how not to die"
they stay quiet, hugthecoast
watch the horizon of the water
and wait for one to fight one's way
through the water
to where the boat is tied off
one has to throw one's self
into the rush
before the rat
will throw a rope.

In order to swim the river
one must enter the river barefoot
the water will be thick-mud-murky
and one won't be able
to see the bottom
one will be pushed
into the vortex
of submerged trees
and caught driftwood
one's legs will be taken

by the mimosa undertow, one will
face the force of the current head
on, one will take a stand
against the inevitable.

Above one is the sun
and the vulture, high on thermals
and mirrored
on the rippling: wings still
as one's fingers in through
the water ricocheting
off the foam of the rapids.

In order to swim the river one
must both be very strong
and one must also know
when to give up
one must watch and feel
the moving surface
& also one must learn
the undercurrents
one will be tossed
about, into and against
one will be a
scarecrow straw
against the water, one
will spin from one's
tenuous toehold in
the sandy mud
spin out past
past where one
can swim back from.

taking
one
step
could
shatter
one
into
pieces.

One
began
believ-
ing
new
things
about
the
world.
one:
that
one
was
dead.

two:
that
one
was
dead.

three:
that
one
was
dead.

YOU'LL
BE
DEAD.

it's ok

One
began
believ-
ing
that
the
weight
of
the
atmo-
sphere
would
crush
one's
bones
to
dust.

One
would
call
it
crush
injury
but
not
know
that
what

Decapitation: Samson

Daddy walked away that day
by being carried away
on a gurney
and taken to the mortuary
taken to the funeral home
where it was a closed casket
and he was buried
in the Ozark home cemetery
on great grandmother's
Old Land
with the tombstone
over top of the grave
it said:

"here lies one who stopped
to smell the roses"

They had a picture of his horse,
Toby, on the tombstone, too.
They didn't let the little girl
attend because no one wanted
to tell the little girl
that father'd killed himself
doing lines of coke with a woman
daddy chosen over one's own mother.

People didn't think
of other ways
to tell the little girl.

People didn't talk to each other
to think about the little girl,
to come up with a story
they could all tell.

People just all stayed silent
to the little girl until she was 40,
but that's another story.

It wasn't their fault,
they all LOST Their Heads
over losing the one they were
head over heels for, their
most darling one
their brilliant one
the most treasured
the brightest star
the one they were so proud of
and that's what made them hate him.

They kept all talking about how
he'd been LOST and how they all
must beg for god to forgive
poor, great Samson and how he
was a LOST soul and everyone wept
loudly except for the best friend,
the Scarecrow.

It's true he
ruffled more than feathers when
he told Samson's parents to
FUCK OFF

doctor
kennedy
would
call
it
was
dis-
socia-
tion
and
how
I
was
dead
for
a
solid
three
months,
like
father
like
daugh-
ter.

bs
srk
ne
ss
boss
reek
brenk
one
sober
sons

you
never
did
know
when
to
shut
your
fucking
mouth

I
disso-
ciated
for
years

the
helmet
pro-
tected
against
a
head
shot
which
was
fatal

like
father
like
daugh-
ter
like

it's true he also made the aunts
and fiances proud
for standing up for the decapitated
coke-sniffing man
in the closed casket.

Everyone except
the little orphan Dorothy,
'cuz she wasn't there
and that's how they all
forgot her.

She began believing
that because her
daddy was dead
and he was
part of her
she was
partly
dead,
too.

Don't Lose Your Head

Our little girl
all grown up
they call her
a headhunter
she keeps these relics
these faces
these stories
these Minds
these bodies' minds
on a chain
that's clinking after her.

Clinking all the time
clacking and throbbing
and dripping pus and stinking up
the room her baggage
is a sequence of heads without
bodies each still mouthing
their hatred, their car wrecks
welding their stories, their secrets
each still projecting their loss
into the future each of them
Whispering like a additional mouth
inside the back of her head until
she doesn't know which way is up
until she's head-over-heels with
confusion until she's a child again
LOSING HER HEAD
trying to figure out who to mind.

it's ok
it's
ok
it's ok
it's
ok
it's ok
it's
ok
it's ok
it's
ok
it's ok
it's
ok
it's ok
it's
ok
it's ok
it's
ok
it's ok
it's
ok
it's ok
it's
ok
it's ok
it's
ok
it's ok
it's
ok
it's ok
it's

ok

it's
ok
to
die

star
fuck

(cuz
we
all
have
wings

but

some
of
us
don't
know
why)

Some-
thing
in-
side
me
broke
I
was
all
alone.

Don't lose your head
you'll get by
in the end.

Don't lose your head, my friend.
Don't Lose Your Head, my friend.

YOU'LL
BE
DEAD.
DEAD.
DEAD.
DEAD.
DEAD.
DEAD.
DEAD.
DEAD.
DEAD.
DEAD.
DEAD.
DEAD.
DEAD.
DEAD.
DEAD.
DEAD.
DEAD.
DEAD.
DEAD.
DEAD.

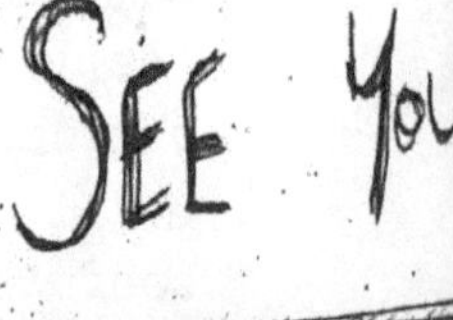

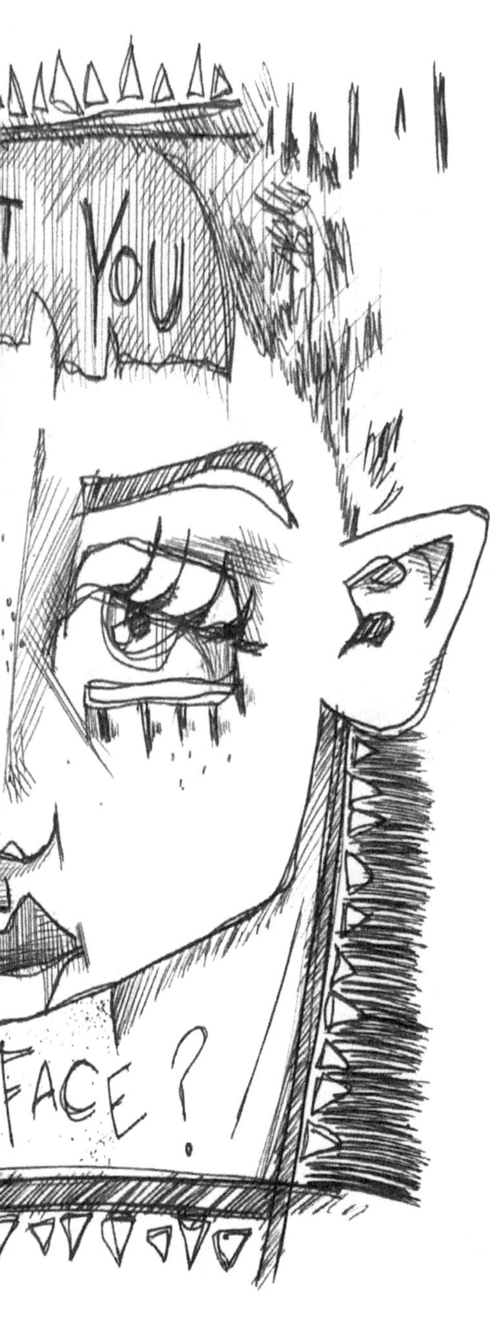

DEAD.
DEAD.
DEAD.
DEAD.
DEAD.
DEAD.
DEAD.
DEAD.
DEAD.
DEAD.
DEAD.
DEAD.
DEAD.
DEAD.
DEAD.
DEAD.
DEAD.
DEAD.
DEAD.
DEAD.
DEAD.
DEAD.
DEAD.
DEAD.
DEAD.
DEAD.
DEAD.
DEAD.
DEAD.
DEAD.
DEAD.

alone.
alone.
alone.
alone.
alone.
alone.
alone.
alone.
alone.
alone.
alone.
alone.
alone.
alone.
alone.
alone.
alone.
alone.
alone.
alone.
alone.
alone.
alone.
alone.
alone.
alone.
alone.
alone.
alone.
alone.
alone.
alone.
alone.
alone.
alone.

alone.
alone.
alone.
alone.
alone.
alone.
alone.
alone.
alone.
alone.
alone.
alone.
alone.
alone.
alone.
alone.
alone.
alone.
alone.
alone.
alone.
alone.
alone.
alone.
alone.
alone.
alone.
alone.
alone.
alone.
alone.
alone.
alone.

orphan.

DEAD.
DEAD.
DEAD.
DEAD.
DEAD.
DEAD.
DEAD.
DEAD.
DEAD.
DEAD.
DEAD.
DEAD.
DEAD.
DEAD.
DEAD.
DEAD.
DEAD.
DEAD.
DEAD.
DEAD.
DEAD.
DEAD.
DEAD.
DEAD.
DEAD.
DEAD.

it's ok.
here I am.

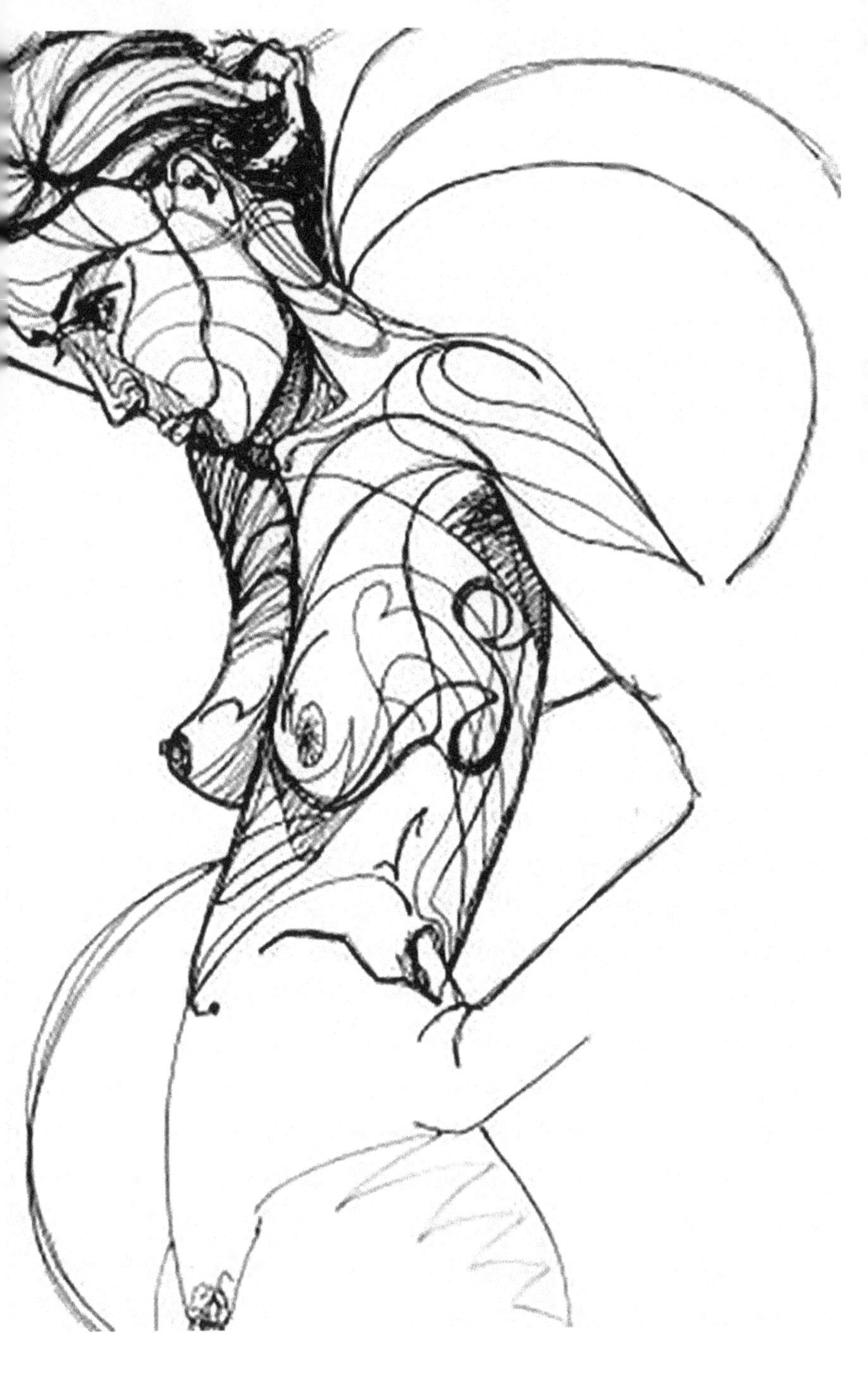

also by

jeanette powers:

Absolute Futility
WTF Press

Earthworms & Stars
Spartan Press

Tiny Chasm
39 West Press

Novel Cliche
39 West Press

The Cosmic Lost and Found
Cringe-Worthy Poets

Perfectly Good Muses:
the collected apologies of JP
Spartan Press

Gasconade
NightBallet Press

contact: jeanettepowers.com
@novel_cliche @drawwithyoureyesclosed
stubbornmulepress@gmail.com

my underwood
font by
mtension

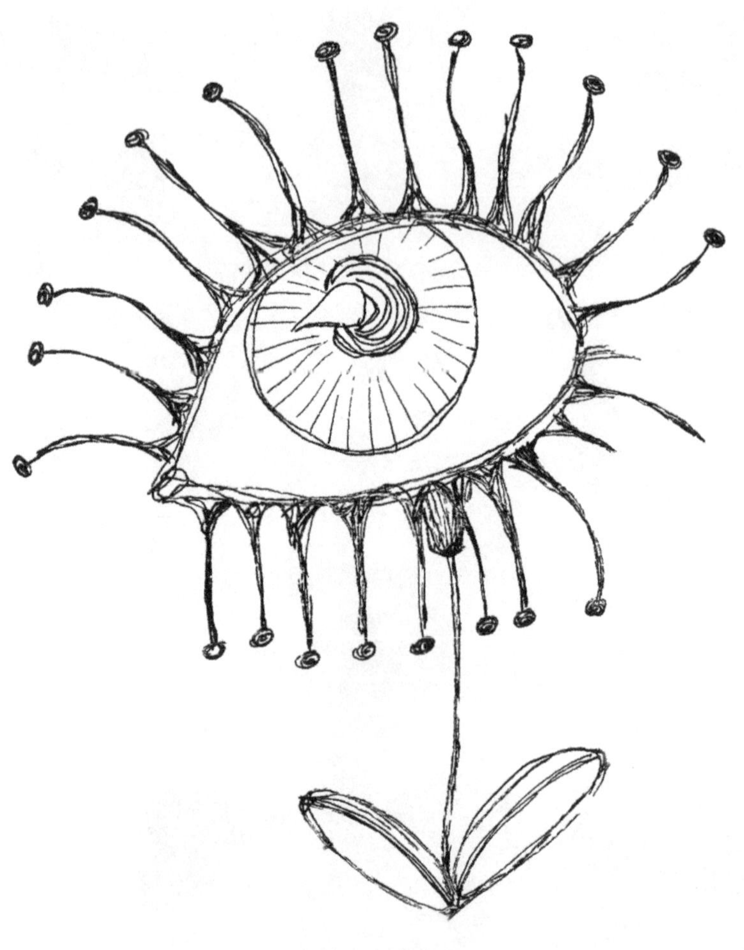

Solidarity.

Printed in the USA
CPSIA information can be obtained
at www.ICGtesting.com
LVHW092009300124
770322LV00004B/146

9 780998 507743